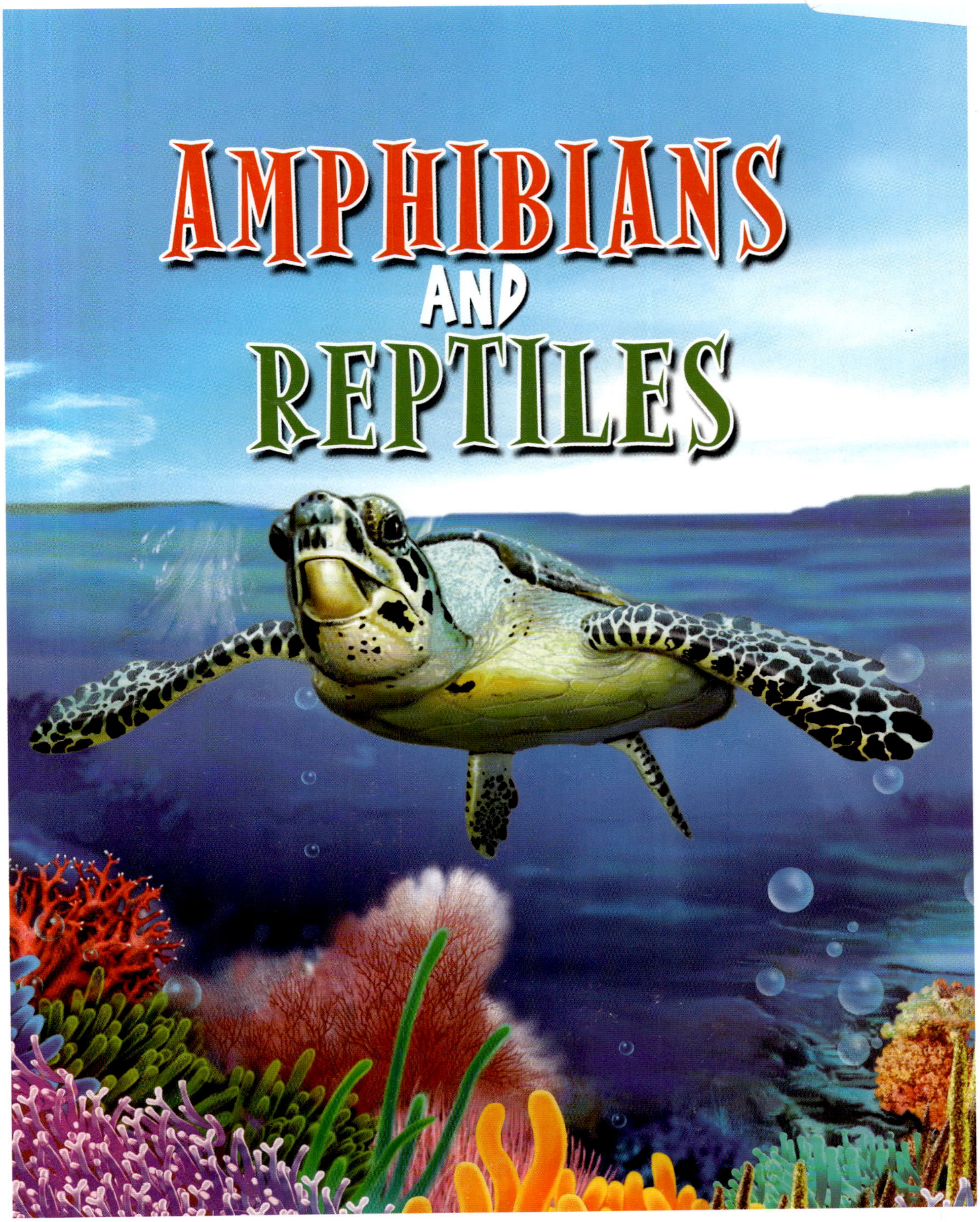
AMPHIBIANS
AND
REPTILES

India Office: A-81, Sector V, Noida- 201301
Email: info@hellofriendbooks.com
Website: www.hellofriendbooks.com

Creative Head:
Sanjay Dhiman

Senior Editor:
Eman Chowdhary

Art Director:
Priyabrata Roy Chowdhury

Content Development:
Wordworx Team
Kirti Kaul

Edited by:
Arpita Barua
Pallavi Sah

Designed by:
Ravinder Singh

Illustrated by:
Chandoo, Rakesh Gurung, Rajendra Nath, Rajeev, Manoj, Vikash,
Prince, Sijoy, Om, Babu, Mohan, Dheeraj and Susanta Kar

ISBN: 81-87108-12-6
Published in 2007 by Om Books International, 4379/4B Prakash House,
Ansari Road, Darya Ganj, New Delhi 110 002, India
Tel.: 91 11 23263363/23265303. email : sales@ombooks.com

CONTENTS

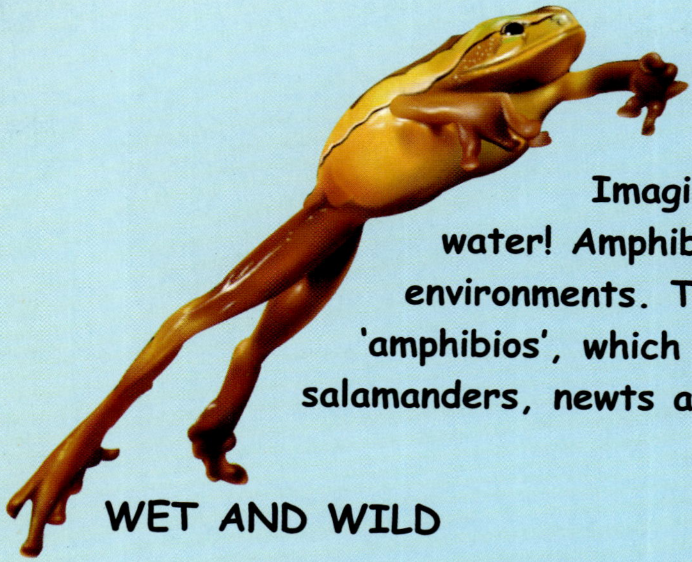

WORLD OF AMPHIBIANS

Imagine a life spent half on land and half in water! Amphibians are animals that can exist in both environments. They were named after the Greek word 'amphibios', which means 'both lives'. Frogs, toads, salamanders, newts and caecilians are all amphibians.

WET AND WILD

Most amphibians spend their baby days in water and grow up to live on land. Some, however, live in water all their lives. Amphibians have the same body temperature as their environment. They have moist skin, which does not dry up even while they are on land. Many amphibians breathe through their skin, though some might have gills in their younger years. An amphibian's body does not have any hair, scales or feathers.

Strawberry Poison Dart frog

Western Green Tree frog

Yellow Eyed Ensatina salamander

Tadpoles

Eggs

WORD-O-LOGY

ENVIRONMENT: *Environment is the area in which something lives or exists.*

BABY DAYS

Most amphibian babies look completely different from their parents. For instance, baby frogs and toads have tails and swim in water, while their parents have legs and mostly live on land. Others, like baby newts and salamanders, resemble their parents.

WATER EGGS

Baby amphibians are born from eggs that their mothers lay, mostly in water. Some mothers hide their eggs so that other animals cannot find and eat them. Interestingly, the Midwife toads carry the eggs on their backs.

FACTASTIC!

The earliest amphibian-like animals lived on Earth about 390 million years ago!

The eyes and nose of a frog are on top of its head, so that it can breathe and see when most of its body is under the water.

A FROG'S FABLE

Mother frogs lay about 100 eggs at a time. These eggs, called frogspawn, are clumped together. They look like little jelly balls with a black eye in the centre of each egg. Since many animals like to eat these eggs, mother frogs keep them safe. While some mothers carry the eggs on their back, some fathers hide them in their vocal sac. Sometimes, frogspawn floats in ponds or sticks to plants.

INSIDE THE EGG

As the days go by, the little black eye inside the egg begins to grow. It soon forms the shape of a head and a tail and grows into a baby frog, called a tadpole. It takes the tadpole about ten days to wriggle out of the white jelly. At this stage, the tadpole is too weak to swim far into the water.

GROWING UP

The little tadpole soon develops external gills to breathe. In the fourth week, the gills are developed within the body. At eight weeks, two tiny bumps come out near the tail. These bumps soon grow into hind legs. The tadpole's tail also gradually disappears. By now, the tadpole has two front legs, like its parents.

Life cycle of frog

WORD-O-LOGY

METAMORPHOSIS: *Metamorphosis is the process in which a tadpole is changed into a frog.*

OUT OF WATER

Soon the tadpole's gills change into developed lungs. This helps them to swim to the surface and gulp in air. The metamorphosis of the frog thus gets complete.

LEAVING THE POND

The little frog now lives on land–at the edge of the pond, under moist stones or on leaves. It swims in the pond but returns to its home on land. It always stays cautious to be away from predators. Waterbirds, such as herons, are specially fond of frogs!

Normally, the life cycle of a frog gets complete between 12-16 weeks, but some frogs that live in colder places or in higher altitudes take a whole winter to go through the tadpole stage.

FACTASTIC!

The Gastric Brooding mother frog swallows her eggs. The tadpoles grow inside the mother's tummy. They come out of the mouth as tiny frogs!

HOP AND SKIP

Have you ever seen a frog? Look near the wettest patch in the garden or near a watering hole in the woods. Here, you are likely to find a frog hopping about on its strong hind legs or swimming expertly using its webbed feet. Its skin is moist, even slimy, and it has large, bulging eyes. Can you hear it sing? The 'song' may be a mating call to attract female frogs or a warning call for other frogs.

Tomato frog

FAMILY TREE

Another animal related to the frog is the toad. It generally lives in dry areas. It has dry, warty skin and a stubby body with short, hind legs. A common toad does not have the frog's balloon-like vocal sac.

TOP TRICKS

Most frogs and toads have patterned skin that helps them blend with their surroundings. The Solomon Island Leaf frogs are coloured and shaped like pointed, dry leaves. This enables them to protect themselves from predators, such as lizards, snakes, hedgehogs, preying birds and large fish.

COLOUR ME RED

Not all frogs and toads like to blend with their surroundings. Some are so brightly coloured that they cannot be missed. Others like to flash their bright bellies when in danger. The bright reds, blues, yellows and purples on their skin are a warning to predators that these animals are not food but are poisonous!

Dwarf Tree frog

The skin of a frog reflects an equal amount of ultraviolet light as its immediate surroundings. In this way, it can protect itself from snakes and other predators.

WORD-O-LOGY

VOCAL SAC: *The bag-like, expandable structure below the throat of the male frog is known as the vocal sac. It is used by the male for mating calls.*

FACTASTIC!

When threatened, Tomato frogs puff themselves up with air, so that they appear too big to be swallowed!

SLIPPERY SALAMANDERS

While you may have often seen frogs and toads, you might not have ever spotted a salamander. This shy creature prefers to leave its home only at night and likes to stay away from people. Although an amphibian, it looks completely different from frogs and toads.

LIZARD OR NOT?

A salamander looks like a lizard. It has four short limbs and a very long tail. Like a lizard, it can also regenerate some of its body parts. This means that if it loses its legs or tail, it can grow them back in a few days. A salamander can also regenerate parts of its heart and eyes!

But on a closer look, a salamander is very different from a lizard. It has smooth, moist skin, unlike the dry, rough skin of a lizard. A salamander also does not have any scales, feathers or hair on its skin.

The largest salamander, the Chinese Giant salamander, is fully aquatic. It grows upto 1.8 metres in length.

Spotted salamander

WORD-O-LOGY

SCALES: *Scales are dead skin cells that look like flakes or dry skin.*

HOME SWEET HOME

As babies, most salamanders live in water. Some continue to stay in water even after they have grown up, as they can never live very far away from water. They generally stay in moist areas, such as under green logs, rocks or near streams. These animals also like to live in shade, and normally come out after sunset. This is why you will never find a salamander basking in the sun. This habit makes them nocturnal animals.

WHAT'S FOR DINNER?

All salamanders hunt other animals for food. Their diet includes small water insects, fish, frogs, frog eggs and even other salamanders!

FACTASTIC!

Salamanders do not make any sound at all. They are completely voiceless animals.

UNUSUAL AMPHIBIANS

NEWTS

Small, bright coloured and semiaquatic, newts can be found in North America, Europe and North Asia. They are, perhaps, the most well-known example of creatures, who can regenerate limbs, eyes and even the spinal cord. Newts are distinguished from the other members of the salamander family by their lack of ribs, or costal grooves, along the sides of the body.

Newts are unique among amphibians because of their three distinct phases of life cycle: aquatic larval stage, immature terrestrial eft stage and aquatic adult stage.

DEFENCE MECHANISM

Many newts produce toxins in the secretions from their skin, as a defence mechanism against predators. Taricha newts of Western North America can produce toxins that can kill humans, if swallowed by mistake.

FACTASTIC!

Smooth newts have been observed to become excited and aggressive at the site of other newts feeding.

WORD-O-LOGY

TOXIN: *Toxin is a poison produced by certain animals, plants or bacteria.*

CAECILIANS

The word 'caecilian' is derived from the Latin word 'caecus', which means blind. These underground dwellers have small eyes that are covered with a layer of skin for protection. This leads to the misconception that they are blind. Caecilians resemble earthworms and snakes.

ANATOMY

The smaller species of the caecilians resemble worms, while the larger species that are almost 1.5 metres in length, resemble snakes. These amphibians are also characterised by a short tail and smooth dark skin. However, some may also have colourful skin. Since their eyes are covered, their visual sense is limited. All caecilians have two tentacles at their head, used for 'olfaction' (act of smelling). They help to detect chemicals dissolved in the air. This is in addition to the normal sense of smell based in their nose.

Eggs

Caecilian

THE WORLD OF REPTILES

Snakes, lizards, crocodiles and turtles—they are creatures that look completely different from one another. While snakes do not have arms or legs, lizards and crocodiles have short legs and a tail. Turtles have a hard shell on their back. Despite their differences, these varied animals belong to the same family—reptiles. Other than snakes, lizards, crocodiles and tortoises, the reptile family also includes the shy tuataras of New Zealand.

SCALY STORY

Generally, a reptile's skin is rough and scaly. It never has any hair or feathers on it. For instance, the crocodiles have hard and bony scales, arranged like armour on their back. While in tortoises, the bony scales fuse to form a tough shell on the back.

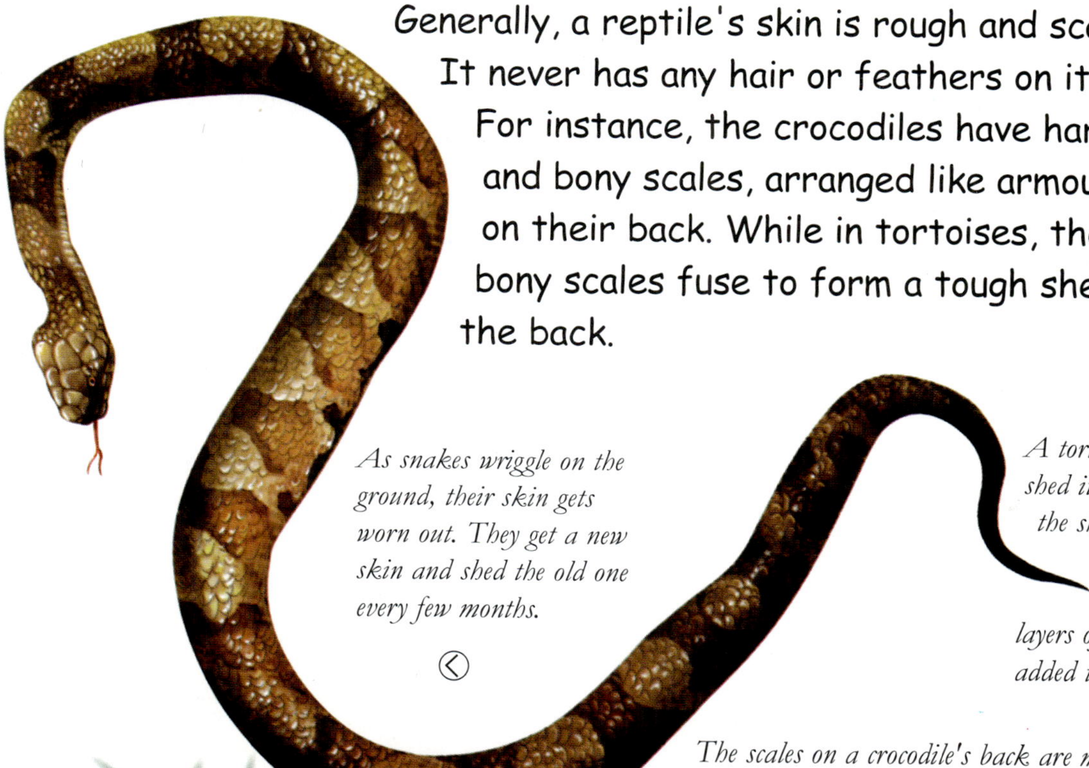

As snakes wriggle on the ground, their skin gets worn out. They get a new skin and shed the old one every few months.

A tortoise does not shed its shell; instead, the shell becomes harder with time, as new layers of keratin are added to it.

The scales on a crocodile's back are made of keratin—the same substance that makes your hair, nails and skin.

WORD-O-LOGY

TUATARA: *A spiny, lizard-like reptile of the coastal islands of New Zealand.*

SUNBATHERS

Amphibians and reptiles are cold-blooded. This means that their body temperature changes with their surroundings. Thus, during the daytime, most reptiles like to sun themselves for a while and make their bodies warm before moving into the shade. But in deserts, snakes and lizards bury themselves in the sand to avoid the harsh sun. During winters, many reptiles go for a long sleep to escape the severe cold. The only place where reptiles do not live is the coldest continent, Antarctica.

Some lizards change their colour as they bask in the sun; they are dark in the morning when it is cold and grow lighter as they absorb the sun's warm rays.

FACTASTIC!

While the largest reptile, the saltwater crocodile, stretches over six metres in length; the smallest one, the dwarf gecko, is smaller than an average human thumb. If a saltwater crocodile could stand on the tip of its tail, it would be taller than a giraffe!

DANGER IN WATER

Crocodiles and alligators are amongst the fiercest hunters ever to have lived on our planet. Another reptile that resembles them in body and behaviour is the gharial, found only in the Indian subcontinent. The earliest ancestors of these reptiles lived around 250 million years ago, when dinosaurs walked the Earth. Their body has not changed much in all these years. For this reason, they are sometimes called 'living fossils'.

BIG AND STRONG

Crocodiles and alligators have tough skin that acts like an armour. They have strong bony plates that become thicker with time. These animals reach the length of about four to six metres—almost as long as two tennis tables, joined from end to end! The biggest crocodiles, the estuarine crocodiles, are sometimes seven metres long—almost the width of an Olympic-sized swimming pool!

A mother crocodile attacks anybody, who goes near her clutch of eggs.

BABY DAYS

Mother crocodiles lay their eggs in a nest on land. When baby crocodiles (called hatchlings) are ready to leave the eggs, they squeak to call the mother. She, then, carries the hatchlings gently in her mouth and releases them in water. Baby crocodiles grow in large nursery groups called pods.

MEAT AND MORE

Crocodiles and alligators are not fussy eaters. They can survive on any animal or bird. They fish or lunge out of water to grab animals from the water's edge. In one single meal, a crocodile can easily eat a zebra, a wildebeast, a heron or even a human being!

FACTASTIC!

In extreme conditions, a crocodile can go without a meal for as long as two years!

WORD-O-LOGY

ESTUARINE: *Estuarine means relating to an estuary, which is that part of the mouth of a river, where it meets the sea tide.*

A TURTLE'S TALE

A turtle spends its life in or near water. For most of its time, it stays on the beaches that are rich in algae and small animals. This is to ensure that there is ample food for them. So, these beaches are called feeding beaches. For breeding, turtles travel long distances, sometimes several thousand kilometres away in the beach. The beaches, where it lays eggs, are called spawning beaches. These beaches have to be very safe for baby turtles to survive.

HOME FOR EGGS

The green mother turtle drags herself on to the beach and lumbers her way to a safe spot, where she lays her eggs. At this spot, she digs a hole, sits inside the hole and lays about a hundred eggs. Then, she hides the 'nest' by covering it with sand and twigs.

Baby turtles are tiny and have soft carapaces, but they are strong. They crawl towards the sea as soon as they emerge from the eggs.

WORD-O-LOGY

SPAWNING: *Spawning is the process of laying eggs.*

BABIES ARE BORN

Unlike other animals, the mother turtle does not stay to help her babies hatch out of the eggs or to help them grow. She leaves soon after laying the eggs. So, the babies are on their own from the minute they are born. They are born with a special tooth, called egg tooth, which helps them break through the egg shell and come out!

But all baby turtles do not survive to become adults. While many are eaten by hungry crabs on their way to the sea, some are snatched up by birds of prey. Others, who make it to the sea, may be gobbled up by fish and sharks in shallow waters. The remaining lucky ones drift out to the safer parts of the sea, where they can live on seaweed and tiny sea animals.

FACTASTIC!

The leatherback turtle is the world's heaviest turtle, weighing as much as a small car.

SLOW AND STEADY

Another fascinating creature in the world of reptiles is the tortoise. It walks very slowly and carries a heavy shell on its back. It can even pull in its head and legs and hide inside the shell. Its cousins, turtles and terrapins, also have a heavy shell, but they cannot hide inside it. Since turtles and terrapins swim, their shell is much flatter than a tortoise's.

THE FAMILY TREE

There might seem no similarity between a rope-like snake and a stout tortoise. But the truth is that lizards, snakes and tortoises are all reptiles. Tortoises, turtles and terrapins are also called chelonians. All chelonians have a carapace and a beak-like mouth. The carapace of the tortoises is dome-shaped and is very tough and hard. This is to protect them from the jaws and paws of predators. The Pancake Tortoise of East Africa is unique. When threatened, it does not withdraw itself into the shell but wedges itself between narrow rocks. It, then, inflates itself with air to make extraction almost impossible for its enemies.

WORD-O-LOGY

CARAPACE: *Carapace is the heavy shell that covers a chelonian's back.*

HOME LIFE

Like all chelonians, even tortoises cannot bear extreme heat or cold. They like to stay sufficiently warm. In cold places, they sit in the sun. In hot places, they bury themselves under the ground for most of the day or wallow in muddy water. These animals walk very slowly, taking several minutes to take a single step!

The carapace of the Three-toed Box turtle is fairly high and is variable in colour. It is usually olive or tan coloured, but some of them may have marked patterns. The skin is brownish, and the forelimbs and the head have yellow or orangish spots.

FACTASTIC!

A tortoise can live as long as 150 years.

BELIEVE IT OR NOT!

Some frogs, like the African clawed toad, have claws.

Some toads get more than half the water they need through a baggy patch on their pelvis, which is pressed against moist surfaces.

The shell of a turtle is made up of 60 different bones, all connected together.

Turtles vary greatly in size and weight. For example, the size of a Bog turtle is 4 inches, while a Leathery turtle weighs as much as 1500 pound!

Did you know that snakes can swallow prey thrice their own size? They do this using their highly stretchable tendons.

The smallest crocodile, the Congo dwarf crocodile, averages one metre in length.

THE LIFE OF A LIZARD

Another popular creature of the reptile family is the lizard. You might have spotted it on a tree on a warm day. It was probably almost the colour of the tree. Or, you might even have seen it on a wall. Did you know that many people welcome lizards into their homes to get rid of flies and other insects?

TRUE REPTILE

A lizard usually has dry, scaly skin. But some lizards, like the Skink, have shiny scales on their body. These scales make their skin appear moist. Skinks look a lot like snakes, as they have very small limbs. But unlike snakes, they have eyelids and ear openings. Lizards do not have ears that stick out like other animals'. Instead, they have a slit-like opening in their head to connect to the inner, hidden eardrum. Lizards live on trees, in marshes, grasslands and forests. They have claws to grip the ground. The gecko has over 1,50,000 fine hooked hair on each toe which gives it a special ability to 'stick' to the surface.

TAIL TALE

Different animals fool their enemies in different ways. When in danger, a lizard can shake off its tail from its body. As the enemy is fooled by the wriggling tail on the ground, the lizard quickly darts to safety. Its body grows a new tail in just a few days.

FACTASTIC!

A chameleon's sticky tongue is longer than its body! The chameleon shoots it out, catches food on it, and rolls it back into the mouth in just a few seconds.

Nile monitors live in Africa, and as the name suggests, they are found near the Nile. They have their nostrils placed high on the snout, which shows that these animals are highly aquatic. They are also excellent climbers and quick runners.

WORD-O-LOGY

MARSH: *Marsh is a kind of wetland having grasses, rushes and reeds on it.*

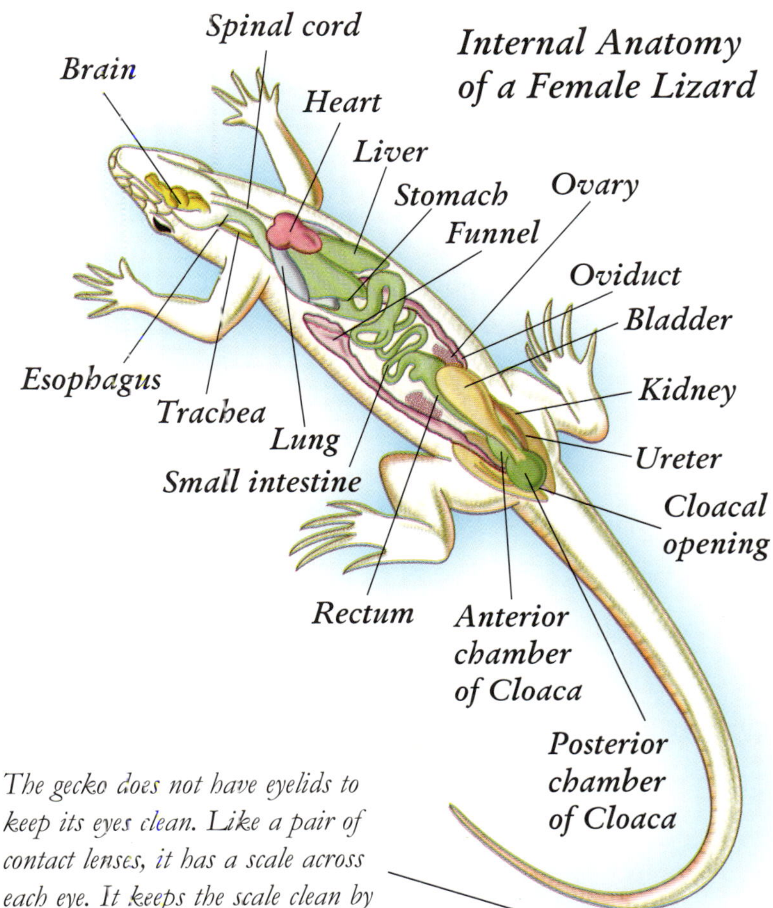

Internal Anatomy of a Female Lizard

The gecko does not have eyelids to keep its eyes clean. Like a pair of contact lenses, it has a scale across each eye. It keeps the scale clean by wiping it with its tongue. How's that for a handy wipe?

Normally chameleons are almost flat. They can rotate each eye and look in two different directions at the same time.

LETHAL LIZARDS

The lizard that you may have seen in your garden is harmless. It eats mostly insects and helps to keep the area free of pests. But not all lizards are harmless. Some are poisonous and use their venom to kill their prey. Most poisonous lizards are among the largest in the world. They are strong and do not have many natural enemies.

BIG AND STRONG

The Komodo dragon does not breathe fire, but it is named after the fire-breathing monster because of its fearful appearance. It is a kind of monitor lizard and has very sharp claws and a tail as long as its body. It has jagged, razor-sharp teeth with which it bites its victims. The poison in its saliva infects the prey and kills it either instantly or after a few days. The Komodo dragon picks the scent of already dead or dying prey and rushes to eat it.

The Gila monster is named after the Gila River Basin in Arizona, USA.

Mexican Beaded lizards are poisonous. Earlier, people thought that only these and Gila monsters were poisonous. They later found that some iguanas and monitor lizards also poison their prey.

WORD-O-LOGY

CARCASS: *Carcass is the body of a dead animal.*

MONSTERS IN THE WILD

Like the Komodo dragon, the Gila (pronounced 'hila') monster has poison in the grooves of its teeth. It bites its victim to inject it with venom, and then chews it to mix the venom in its blood. Baby rats, birds and reptile eggs are its favourite food.

FACTASTIC!

In earlier times, people thought that some lizards (like Komodo dragons) were a warning of the presence of crocodiles in the area. Hence, they called them 'monitor' lizards.

The Komodo dragon, the largest lizard in the world, lives on various islands (including Komodo, after which it is named) in Indonesia. This monitor lizard eats animal carcass or wild pigs, goats, deer, water buffaloes and even smaller Komodo dragons.

Perentie, the Australian monitor lizard, is an agile hunter and even eats baby kangaroos.

UNUSUAL LIZARDS

Have you ever heard about a flying lizard or one with a frill around its neck? These are not imaginary creatures. Such extraordinary creatures do exist. These fascinating features help them to scare away enemies. These are their defence mechanisms.

Like other lizards, the slow worm can shed its tail, but it cannot grow it back completely.

THE FLYER

Lizards usually do not fly. But there are some special lizards, which do. These flying lizards have two flaps of skin on either side of their body. The flaps act as wings and help the lizards glide in air and swoop over their prey.

LIZARD OR NOT?

The Horned Toad of North America is not a toad but a lizard. This lizard has a toad's squatty body and two horns above its eyes. The Slow Worm is another lizard that does not resemble the rest of its family. Instead, it looks like a snake. It has no limbs, but a snake-like, shiny body. But unlike a snake, it has eyelids.

PRICKLY BALL

The African Armadillo lizard has a spiny body, except for its soft belly. It is brown in colour and has a distinctive curled up defensive posture. It grows upto 10 inches in length.

When in danger, an Armadillo lizard rolls itself up into a ball by holding its tail in its jaws and hiding its belly behind its sharp scales and spines.

WORD-O-LOGY

DEFENCE MECHANISM: Defence mechanism is a feature by which any creature protects itself from its enemies.

When a Horned Toad is threatened, it squirts blood from its eyes. Its favourite food is ants, but it also eats crickets, beetles, pill bugs etc. It can eat over 200 ants in a day.

FACTASTIC!

A Stump-tailed skink is very hard to catch, as its tail looks like its head. This makes it difficult for the enemy to know if the skink is coming or going!

The Australian Frilled lizard plays a bluff game when it is threatened. It opens up the frill around its neck, hisses and jumps at its enemy to scare it away.

SLITHERING SNAKES

A snake belongs to the same family as the tortoise but it looks completely unlike one. It does not have the tortoise's shell or its stocky limbs. In fact, a snake has no limbs at all. It looks like a tail with a mouth. You probably think that all snakes are the same. However, you will be surprised to know that there are over 2,500 different types of snakes in the world. While some of these are poisonous, others kill their prey by wrapping themselves tightly around it. Most snakes live on land, but some live in rivers, lakes or even seas.

NEW SKIN

When a snake grows, it becomes long and thick. Due to this, its skin stretches. Since it slithers on the ground, the skin gets rough and damaged. To keep it shiny, clean and of the right size for the body, the snake sheds its skin regularly. This process is called moulting. A new skin grows in place of the one that is shed.

Unlike other snakes, the Peringuey's adder from Namibia moves sidewards and leaves a unique trail in the sand.

WORD-O-LOGY

TRAIL: *Trail is a mark left by something that has passed over a surface.*

NO BACKBONE?

Looking at a snake, you might think that it has no bones. It seems to squeeze its way through the tiniest of cracks in the ground or on trees. But the truth is that a snake has more bones in its back than any other animal. These bones, called vertebrae, are linked to one another by thousands of muscles. The snake can move these muscles to crawl in various ways—sideways, winding to and fro and moving in big loops.

TEETH OR NO TEETH?

Some snakes do not have teeth at all, while others have very sharp ones. They do not use these teeth to tear or chew their food. They use them for gripping their prey, which they swallow whole. Poisonous snakes have a pair of sharp and long teeth, called fangs, with which they inject poison into their prey.

FACTASTIC!

Snakes dart out their forked tongue to pick up and recognise their prey's scent.

POISONOUS PREDATORS

Australian taipan

Alligators and crocodiles grab their prey and tear it to pieces before swallowing it. Many lizards sting their prey to stun it. Snakes, on the other hand, employ a different method to catch food. Many of them inject poison into their prey. The poison does not always kill the prey; it can cause blindness, muscle weakness, paralysis and, sometimes, death. The world's most poisonous snakes belong to a family called elapids, which includes cobras, mambas, taipans and sea snakes. Other poisonous snakes include vipers and adders.

Gaboon viper

SPITTING SNAKES

While some cobras bite their victims to inject them with poison, 'spitting' cobras spray poison at their prey. They aim for the prey's eyes, which causes sharp pain and even blindness. These snakes do not attack people, except when threatened. Just two ounce of a King cobra's venom is enough to kill 20 people!

Mamba

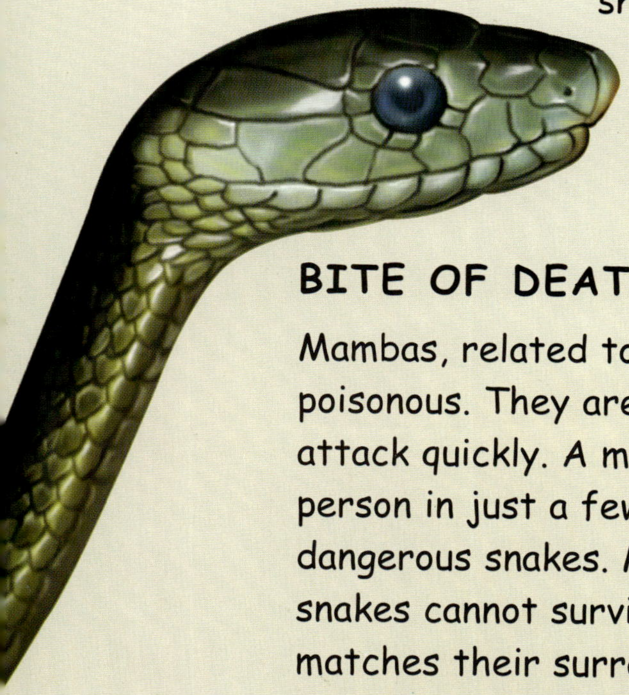

BITE OF DEATH

Mambas, related to cobras, are also highly poisonous. They are nervous snakes and attack quickly. A mamba's bite, if left untreated, can kill a person in just a few hours. Adders and vipers are also very dangerous snakes. Many adders live in cold places, where other snakes cannot survive. These reptiles camouflage well, as their skin matches their surroundings. Mambas, if cornered, strike repeatedly. It is said that they have even brought down a baby giraffe and a lion with their venom.

WORD-O-LOGY

PARALYSIS: *Paralysis is the inability to move a part of the body.*

When threatened, the King cobra spreads out its hood and rises off the ground to look at the enemy in the eye. The hood of the Indian cobra has eyespots, which look like a pair of spectacles. King cobras are famous for their complex and unique parental care. A pair of King cobras help each other to find a suitable nesting spot. In spite of having no limbs, the female snake scoops dead leaves around with its long body and makes a nest.

FACTASTIC!

The world's most venomous snake, the Belcher's sea snake, is said to be 100 times deadlier than even the most poisonous land snake!

COIL AND KILL

All snakes are not poisonous. Some snakes kill their prey by wrapping themselves tightly around it. These snakes are called constrictors. Boas and pythons belong to this family. While some constrictors are just a few inches long, others, like the boa constrictor, can measure over 18 feet. One of the largest snakes in the world, the Anaconda of South America, is a boa constrictor. These snakes have very thick, muscular bodies.

CATCHING FOOD

Pythons and boas cannot see very well. Instead, they use their tongue to sense the scent of their surroundings. They dart their forked tongue in and out to detect food. They also have heat sensors near their nostrils to locate warm-blooded animals. Boas and pythons also have heat pits located on their heads. These temperature-sensing organs are so sensitive that the snakes can effectively sense even a slight change of 0.002° Celsius. This helps them to navigate and find their prey in the dark.

WORD-O-LOGY

SQUASH: *Squash means to squeeze or compress something by force.*

DINNER TIME

Once a constrictor finds its food, it seizes its prey in its jaws, and then, slowly wraps itself around it, until the prey can no longer breathe. Then, it swallows the prey whole. Like other snakes, constrictors do not chew their food. It takes weeks for a constrictor to completely digest a big meal, like an antelope. These snakes can eat rodents, birds, monkeys, lizards and even crocodiles and deer.

BURROWING KILLER

The Woma python of Australia eats mostly rodents. Unlike other pythons and boas, it does not hunt in the open, but in burrows. It does not coil itself around its prey, but squashes its prey against walls and kills it.

Reticulated pythons eat deer, kangaroos and monkeys. They are even known to have eaten humans!

FACTASTIC!

Most snakes have only one working lung. But the constrictors use both their lungs to breathe.

GIANT MOVERS

In ancient times, people created tales of mysterious snake-like monsters that roamed the rivers and seas. These monsters were said to be unbelievably long and heavy. As zoologists studied wildlife, and as science developed, it became known that the ancient people may not have been entirely incorrect. They might have actually seen incredibly large snakes. We now know of snakes that are even longer than the wings of a passenger aircraft. These snakes include giant Anacondas and pythons.

A constrictor's upper jaw is loosely attached to the lower jaw. This enables it to open its mouth wide enough to swallow not only small animals, like a frog, but also animals much larger than itself.

LONG OR SHORT?

Measuring the length of a snake is not easy. When a snake is caught, it tends to coil itself. When it dies, its body stretches a lot, and it looks much longer than it was, when it lived. This makes it almost impossible for scientists to know the exact length of any living snake.

WORD-O-LOGY

ZOOLOGIST: *Zoologist is a person, who specialises in the study of wildlife.*

LONG, LONGER, LONGEST

A snake never stops growing. It continues to grow longer and thicker, even when it is old. The heaviest snake in the world is the Burmese python. It weighs around 200 kilograms, which is almost the weight of a Siberian tiger. Another giant mover is the Reticulated python—the longest-known snake in the world. One Reticulated python from Indonesia is over 32 feet in length!

FACTASTIC!

Unlike most other reptiles, Anacondas do not lay eggs; instead, they give birth to young ones. The mother Anaconda keeps her eggs inside her body, where they hatch. She then pushes the babies out at the right time.

A Royal python, also called a Ball python, is black and brown in colour, with a yellow tan underbelly. It lives for 20-40 years.

LIZARDS OF THE PAST

Dinosaurs first appeared on Earth about 250 million years ago. For over 100 million years, they ruled the planet. Then, they suddenly disappeared. Human beings have never seen a dinosaur but scientists have discovered fossils, which tell them about dinosaurs and their behaviour.

DINOSAUR FAMILY

The dinosaur family comprised of two types of dinosaurs—bird-hipped and lizard-hipped. All bird-hipped dinosaurs were plant-eaters, while lizard-hipped dinosaurs included both, plant and meat-eaters.

BIG AND SMALL

Most dinosaurs were very large. While the smallest dinosaur was probably the size of a chicken, the largest of them weighed about 70 tonnes—an elephant, the largest land mammal today, weighs just about 5 tonnes!

TOOTH TALE

Dinosaurs had different kinds of looks, body and teeth. Some had narrow teeth for chewing leaves. Others had peg-like teeth for crushing food. Most of the plant-eaters swallowed stones and pebbles to grind tough plants in their tummy.

VANISHING ACT

The extinction of the dinosaurs is still a mystery. Some scientists believe that dinosaurs might have died because they had become too big to move without falling over. Some suggest that the climate change in the late Cretaceous Period made survival difficult for the dinosaurs. Another theory says that Earth was hit by a powerful comet, as a result of which, all the dinosaurs died out. Some scientists also believe that there were near-continuous volcanic eruptions on the Earth which led to the death of the dinosaurs.

FACTASTIC!

Plant-eating dinosaurs never grazed, as there was no grass on Earth at the time. The first grass appeared 25 million years after dinosaurs died out.

WORD-O-LOGY

FOSSILS: *Fossils are remains of an animal or plant that lived hundreds of years ago.*

A widely accepted theory is that an asteroid hit Earth some 65 million years ago. The impact would have penetrated the Earth's surface, resulting in a series of volcanic eruptions. The intense heat and lava from these volcanoes would have perished all life forms on Earth.

SOS

Dinosaurs have always intrigued us, but unfortunately, we can never see them in flesh and blood today. Dinosaurs became extinct long ago. Even today, a number of creatures are heading for extinction. Some of them are dying out just because of our carelessness and cruelty. If we do not actively try to save these endangered animals, they will completely die out. In that case, we will not be able to see these animals anywhere—not even in zoos or conservation centres. Endangered amphibians and reptiles include many types of turtles, lizards, snakes and toads.

TURTLES IN DANGER

Among all the turtles, sea turtles are the most threatened. Some species, such as the Green sea turtle, the Hawksbill, the Leatherback and the Loggerhead sea turtles are facing real challenges to survive. Turtles are hunted for their beautiful shells, meat and eggs. Turtles are also dying because there are very few safe beaches left for them to lay their eggs on.

Loggerhead turtles were widely hunted for their fat, which was used to make cosmetics. Killing these animals is now banned by law.

American crocodile

Californian garter snake

Leopard tortoise

WORD-O-LOGY

HABITAT: *Habitat refers to the natural home of an animal.*

GIANT LOSS

The largest lizard in the world may die out in a few years. There are just about 6,000 Komodo dragons left in the world. The giant Galapagos tortoises are also slowly dying out, as other animals and humans damage or steal their eggs and drive them out of their natural home.

SNAKE STORY

While some snakes are facing extinction because their habitat is being encroached upon or taken away, other species are dying because poachers hunt them down for their skin or venom. One of the deadliest snakes in the world, the King cobra, may soon only be a part of legend, as it is highly endangered.

FACTASTIC!

In India, over 10,000 dead Olive Ridley turtles have been washed ashore in the past 10 years! It is believed that they died because the sea water is highly polluted.

Gloves made of turtle's skin

Coat made of snake skin

Boot made of Alligator's skin

ACTIVITY–SPRINGY SNAKES

How about making a snake in your favourite colour? It's very easy and a whole lot of fun!

To make a springy snake, you will need:

- A large paper plate
- Your favourite type of colour (you can use any, like wax, sketch, water etc)
- A sheet of thin cardboard
- A felt pen
- Some glue
- A pair of scissors
- Two small buttons for eyes and some paper for the forked tongue
- A paper punch
- A strand of string

To make the springy snake, all you need to do is:

- Make a spiral pattern on one side of the paper plate, using the felt pen.
- Stick the paper plate on the thin cardboard sheet.
- Cut the cardboard sheet along the edges of the plate.
- Colour the round cardboard piece on both the sides using your favourite colour; you can even draw creative patterns on the cardboard, if you want your snake to have beautiful scales.

- If you have used water colours, let your paint dry.
- Use scissors to cut the cardboard along the spiral pattern that you had drawn on the paper plate. Remember, you must be very careful while doing this!

- Stick the tiny buttons where the snake's eyes should be. The snake's tail is right in the centre of the spiral pattern.
- Cut paper to make the snake's forked tongue.

- Stick the forked tongue to the snake's mouth.
- Punch a hole at the far end of the snake's tail.
- Pass the string through the hole in the tail and tie it on.

Hisssssss! Your springy snake is ready! Now, measure this snake using a measuring tape. How long is it? Compare it to the length of an Anaconda. Which is longer?

TRIVIA

- The scientific study of reptiles and amphibians is called Herpetology.
- A group of frogs is called an army, while a group of toads is called a knot.
- The purple frog, a new specie, was discovered in India, in 2003. This unique frog spends most of the time underground and comes to the surface for two weeks only, when it has to mate.
- Tiger salamanders have no ear glands and no teeth.
- Newts belong to the same family as salamanders. They have the same body features and habits as salamanders. Together, newts and salamanders are called caudates.
- You might have heard tales about raining frogs. These are real events. These happen when a windstorm passes over a pond full of frogs, picking them up and depositing them somewhere else.
- Unlike most turtles, which are not comfortable in cold, the Blanding's turtle has been observed swimming under the ice in the Great Lakes region.
- A Ball python gets its name from the fact that it curls itself into a ball and hides its head, when threatened.
- Before shedding of the skin, the eyes of the snake become blue or milky white. This happens due to lymph-like fluid between the old and the new skin.
- Crocodiles are the most vocal of all the reptiles. Some species can communicate upto 20 different kinds of messages through sound alone.